Judgment

for

Jezebel

A Portfolio of Power
for Next Level Ministry

ISBN 978-0-9975864-1-1

Table of Contents

Dedication

This book is dedicated to the martyrs in the Middle East who died for the Word of God, in particular the 21 Egyptian martyrs who were beheaded in February 2015 at the hands of a Jezebel spirit.

And I saw the woman drunken with the blood of the saints, and with the blood of the martyrs of Jesus: and when I saw her, I wondered with great admiration. - Revelation 17:6 KJV

Introduction

Beloved Readers,

Do you find yourself in an extremely fierce fight for your destiny? Do you find yourself wondering that if God has called me to do this particular task, why am I going through so much? If God has called me to do a certain assignment (which I believe He has), why is there so much constant resistance? You are not alone!

If you have asked some of these questions, this book will help you understand why there is such opposition and why there is a fierce fight devised against your destiny. Additionally, this book will equip you from the Word of God to bring you into the highest dimension of destiny. The discernment you will acquire will enable you to target assignments that could destroy your destiny, or pull you out of your place and spiritual inheritance.

These kinds of battles and struggles are also revealed in many of the lives of "chosen" individuals in the Bible. Their challenges, emotional grief, deep dilemmas, and victories are written in the Bible as God's voice to you, because He foreknew your personal pain and conflict.

The prophet Elijah in particular experienced similar struggles. His primary purpose and assignment from heaven was to confront and subdue the strength of Jezebel in his generation. He also equipped the next generation through Elisha his servant to destroy Jezebel; Elisha then continued this process by teaching "the sons of the prophets" about how to obliterate this evil spirit (2 Kings 9:1-7).

The Bible tells us that Jezebel had obtained illegal rulership over the land of Israel through manipulation, intimidation, and control. In 2 Kings 9:22, the Bible refers to this as "witchcraft."

Jezebel is an anointing assailant. This is a spirit that operates in every generation to kill the prophets and to hijack destinies (1 Kings 18:4). Jezebel is an anointing assailant after those who have been called to do great things for God in this hour. This is why the scripture says in 2 Kings 9:7b to "avenge all the blood of all (God's) servants the prophets, and the blood of all the servants of the Lord, at the hand of Jezebel."

The only thing that will destroy Jezebel is the anointing. This is why Elisha, the servant of Elijah, sent one of the sons of the prophets to anoint Jehu to be the king. Scripture documents details of how an unknown servant was given a box of oil to anoint Jehu to be king. This anointing was to overthrow the government of Ahab and Jezebel (2 King 9:1-7 and 2 Kings 9:22). Similarly, you are also called to challenge this system and to bring it down through the anointing. This book is a manual for ministry designed to equip you to become so close to the Holy Spirit through the anointing that you will overcome every trial, test, and trap set up by Jezebel.

You are the chosen of this generation. Your vision and purpose is so important for God's kingdom to go forward. Just as Elijah challenged Jezebel and destroyed her evil influence over the land, so will your ministry vision and prophetic purpose drive out the powers of darkness and establish God's kingdom. This book is designed with your destiny in mind.

In Christ,

Dr. Michelle Corral+

Judgment for Jezebel

Chapter 1

Our First Love: Avoiding Destiny Detours

Beloved, the purpose of this book is to help all of us fall more in love with the Lord, to keep our fire and passion for Him burning brightly, and to accomplish our highest destiny. In these last days, seducing spirits will try to move us out of our place of ministry and destiny. This book aims to help us identify and overcome any evil spirits that may be subtly trying to move us away from God's perfect plan for our lives, even just a little bit. By applying the principles in this book, we will be empowered to reach our highest pinnacle of purpose.

It is so important that we are in pursuit of the passion of loving Jesus above all things. The following passages of scripture show us how much emphasis the Lord places on passionately loving Him, and how important it is that we keep ourselves from being deceived.

Revelation 2:1-5

[1] Unto the angel of the church of Ephesus write: These things saith he that holdeth the seven stars in his right hand, who walketh in the midst of the seven golden candlesticks; [2] I know thy works, and thy labour, and thy patience, and how thou canst not bear them which are evil: and thou hast tried them which say they are apostles, and are not, and hast found them liars: [3] And hast borne, and hast patience, and for my name's sake hast labored, and hast not fainted. [4] Nevertheless I have somewhat against thee, because thou hast left thy first love. [5] Remember therefore from whence thou art fallen, and repent, and do the first works; or else I will come unto thee quickly, and will remove thy candlestick out of his place, except thou repent.

1 Timothy 4:1 KJV
Now the Spirit speaketh expressly, that in the latter times some shall depart from the faith, giving heed to seducing spirits, and doctrines of devils.

The Greek word "pipto" appears in Revelation 2:4 and means to fall from, to fall out of one's place, or to be brought down to a lower level, while the Greek word "aphistemi" in 1 Timothy 4:1 means to lead away, or to depart from. When we talk about people who have left the faith and have given heed to seducing spirits and doctrines of devils, we may be talking about people who have backslid down to a lower level; these people aren't necessarily reprobate.

In Revelation 2:1-3, Jesus is saying that the church at Ephesus is commendable in many ways. The Lord is telling the believers at Ephesus that they have labored, they have been patient, and they haven't fainted. He also commends them for effectively handling the false apostles that were in their midst.

In many ways, this church is doing an outstanding job when it comes to serving the Lord. However, Jesus is finding fault with the believers at Ephesus because they have left their first love.

Beloved, we need to be very careful that we do not leave our first love. It may be the case that we used to serve the Lord with all our heart, our soul, our mind, and our strength. But now we may be serving Him in a mechanical way. We may be going through the motions of serving God, but we are no longer madly in love with Jesus. Our primary reason for serving the Lord used to be because we loved Him, but now there may be other reasons involved like wanting to maintain a certain position; maybe we like the attention we get from being noticed in church, or maybe we have a hidden agenda. We're still serving God, but we have lost our first love. No! Our primary pursuit and primary passion is to love the Lord above all else. If we don't love the Lord as much as we used to love Him, we need to fall in love with Him again!

Once our love walk with the Lord is not what is used to be, the enemy can begin to affect other areas of our lives, including our destiny. And when we don't fulfill our destinies, other people's lives are negatively affected as well. The Lord has a specific plan and calling for each one of us. When we walk in His perfect will and plan for our lives, it is a blessing to the Lord and to the world around us.

One of the ways that the enemy will try to get us to lower our level of love for the Lord and to move us out of our destinies is by trying to bewitch us. Let's take a look at this concept in the book of Acts.

Acts 8:9 KJV
But there was a certain man called Simon, which beforetime in the same city used sorcery, and bewitched the people of Samaria, giving out that himself was some great one.

Acts 8:11 KJV
And to him they had regard, because that of long time he had bewitched them with sorceries.

The word "bewitch" is "existemi" in Greek, which means to astound, to fascinate, or to make one almost insane. "Ex" means to pull out of, and "stemi" means to stand and refers to one's place. Being bewitched means that we are being pulled out of our place or being pulled out of something, including our ministries. "Existemi" can be compared to mind control; we don't have complete control over our thinking faculties when we are bewitched. Maybe someone came and planted a thought in our minds that wasn't from the Lord; it may have been an angry thought, a self-pitying thought, or a depressing thought. Then the enemy added a little fuel to the fire, and that thought began to grow. We didn't know about spiritual warfare, so we kept thinking that same thought over and over and over again. Before we knew it, that thought had become a stronghold that affected our actions and the rest of our lives.

Our thoughts are like a rudder on a ship. If the enemy can get us thinking about something that's not from the Lord, he can pull us off course and the whole direction of our lives can change. When we are bewitched, we can't hear the Lord and we stop obeying His loving direction for our lives, as we see in the book of Galatians.

Galatians 3:1 KJV
O foolish Galatians, who hath bewitched you, that ye should not obey the truth, before whose eyes Jesus Christ hath been evidently set forth, crucified.

The enemy is subtle: he can sound just like our own voice and start complaining in our soul. He can plant questions like, "Why am I serving God? Does anybody even notice or care?" Sometimes it can be difficult to tell the difference between our own voice and the voice of the enemy. We need to always pray for discernment!

The book of Deuteronomy gives us an overview of the different kinds of spiritual forces that may try to lessen our love for the Lord and move us away from our highest destinies and callings. Let's take a look at these verses so that we are prepared to stay on track with the Lord!

Deuteronomy 18:9-13 KJV
[9] When thou art come into the land which the LORD thy God giveth thee, thou shalt not learn to do after the abominations of those nations. [10] There shall not be found among you any one that maketh his son or his daughter to pass through the fire, or that useth divination, or an observer of times, or an enchanter, or a witch. [11] Or a charmer, or a consulter with familiar spirits, or a wizard, or a necromancer. [12] For all that do these things are an abomination unto the LORD: and because of these abominations the LORD thy God doth drive them out from before thee. [13] Thou shalt be perfect with the LORD thy God.

Let's take a closer look at some of the words used in the above passage from Deuteronomy.

- "Divination" comes from the Hebrew word "qesem" which refers to witchcraft (Strong's Hebrew 7081).
- "Enchanter" comes from the Hebrew word "nachash" which means to practice divination and observe signs (Strong's Hebrew 5172).
- "Witch" derives from the Hebrew word "kashaph" which means to practice sorcery (Strong's Hebrew 3784).
- "Charmer" comes from the Hebrew word "chabar" which means to unite, be joined, charm, and tie a magic knot or spell (Strong's Hebrew 2266).
- "Consulter" derives from the Hebrew word "shaal" which means to ask or inquire (Strong's Hebrew 7592).
- "Wizard" comes from the Hebrew word "yiddeoni" which refers to familiar spirits (Strong's Hebrew 3049).

Putting all of these definitions together, we see that anything that involves seeking guidance from ungodly sources, giving credit to ungodly sources, speaking ungodly words, and making ungodly agreements is a form of witchcraft. Anything which has these characteristics has the power to bewitch us, and we must take spiritual authority over it.

We need to be like Daniel and Joseph, who understood that God is the only One who has all the answers and can provide everything that we need.

Daniel 2:28 KJV

But there is a God in heaven that revealeth secrets and maketh known to the king what shall be in the latter days.

Genesis 41:16 KJV
And Joseph answered Pharaoh, saying, It is not in me: God shall give Pharaoh an answer of peace.

Beloved readers, in the chapters ahead, we will learn how to withstand the wiles of the enemy and give glory to God, in the name of Jesus!

Prayer

Dear Lord,

I ask You to help me make sure that You are always in first place in my life. I break off any spirit that is trying to bewitch me, that is coming against my destiny and anything that God has given me to do. I declare and decree that I will fulfill God's plan for my life, in the name of Jesus!

Diary for Destiny

1. How is your love walk with the Lord? What are your primary reasons for serving Him?

2. Have you ever been "bewitched" by something that tried to pull you away from your destiny? How did you handle the situation? Now that you have read this chapter, how might you have handled the situation differently?

Chapter 2

Breaking the Spell of Jezebel: The Deception of Disguise

Beloved readers, one of the most subtle serpentine spirits that believers can encounter is the spirit of Jezebel. We see this serpentine-like nature of spirits in two descriptions in God's Word:

Genesis 3:1 KJV
Now the serpent was more subtle than any beast of the field.

1 Timothy 4:1 KJV
Now the Spirit speaketh expressly that in the end times some shall depart from the faith, giving heed to seducing spirits and doctrines of devils.

As you may recall, Jezebel makes a grand entrance into the pages of Biblical history as the "unlawful" wife of King Ahab. In 1 Kings 16:30, the text teaches how heaven objected to this unlawful union that would later lead to the downfall of King Ahab and cause a severe famine in the northern kingdom.

1 Kings 16:30-31 KJV
[30] And Ahab the son of Omri did evil in the sight of the Lord, more than all that were before him. [31] And it came to pass, as if it had been a light thing for him to walk in the sins of Jeroboam the son of Nebat, that he took to wife Jezebel, the daughter of Ethbaal king of the Zidonians, and went and served Baal, and worshipped him.

This grand entrance into the pages of scripture prophetically prefigures the struggle with strongholds that we encounter when we are in a battle with the spirit of Jezebel. We need to understand that Jezebel was given in marriage to Ahab through an "affinity" marriage. Oftentimes throughout scripture, we see affinity marriages that took place to increase the national security of Israel. These affinity marriages were done to stabilize the economy and other national interests of Israel. Whenever King David entered into an affinity marriage, the bride converted to worship and serve the God of Israel. We see an example of an affinity marriage between David and Maacah in the book of 2 Samuel.

2 Samuel 3:2-3 KJV
[2] And unto David were sons born in Hebron: and his firstborn was Amnon, of Ahinoam the Jezreelitess; [3] And his second, Chileab, of Abigail the wife of Nabal the Carmelite; and the third, Absalom the son of Maacah the daughter of Talmai king of Geshur.

Note that Maacah, the daughter of Talmai king of Geshur, had to completely convert and accept the laws of God in His Word and serve the God of Israel. We eventually see that Israel conquered the territory of Geshur for God, and His majesty began to spread among the nations.

In clashing contrast, Ahab had no regard for God, no intent to give God glory, and no plan to sanctify God's name among the nations. He was completely pulled into the seducing spirit of Jezebel through the dangling glitter of improving Israel's economy. Jezebel, the daughter of Ethbaal king of the Zidonians, was Phoenician by descent. The people of Phoenicia were known for producing purple dyes, a very expensive commodity in the ancient world. The ancient Phoenicians were a maritime people and were also known for cypress wood, embroidered linen, and the cedars of Lebanon.

In the eyes of Ahab, an affinity marriage with Jezebel from Phoenicia would be a tremendous boost for trade and for Israel's economy. Thus, beloved, we see the spirit of Jezebel gaining entrance into our lives through compromise, rooted in our failure to trust God for everything. We have already set ourselves up, beloved ones, for defeat and downfall when we do not trust God. Let's take a look at the book of Jeremiah for further detail about the importance of trusting in God, not man, to meet all of our needs.

Jeremiah 17:5-8 KJV

[5] Thus saith the LORD; Cursed be the man that trusteth in man, and maketh flesh his arm, and whose heart departeth from the LORD. [6] For he shall be like the heath in the desert, and shall not see when good cometh; but shall inhabit the parched places in the wilderness, in a salt land and not inhabited. [7] Blessed is the man that trusteth in the LORD, and whose hope the LORD is. [8] For he shall be as a tree planted by the waters, and that spreadeth out her roots by the river, and shall not see when heat cometh, but her leaf shall be green; and shall not be careful in the year of drought, neither shall cease from yielding fruit.

This is why, beloved reader, we must have a life of prayer set aside and apart from our lives of ministry. It is very easy for a young novice in ministry who does not understand how important it is to be attached to God in prayer to begin to trust the flesh and place his or her confidence in the flesh.

The Spirit of Subtle Seduction

The spirit of subtle seduction was rampant in the early church, just as it is today. Failure to overcome the spirit of Jezebel was one of the primary problems that we see in the 7 Letters to the 7 Churches revealed in the book of Revelation. This means that the doors of deception can be so strong that we don't even realize we have tolerated instead of obliterated the spirit of Jezebel.

Revelation 2:18-20
[18] And unto the angel of the church in Thyatira write; These things saith the Son of God, who hath his eyes like unto a flame of fire, and his feet are like fine brass; [19] I know thy works, and charity, and service, and faith, and thy patience, and thy works; and the last to be more than the first. [20] Notwithstanding I have a few things against thee, because thou sufferest that woman Jezebel, which calleth herself a prophetess, to teach and to seduce

my servants to commit fornication, and to eat things sacrificed unto idols.

This is a very strong "tochaha" (the Hebrew word for "rebuke") that Jesus is giving to the beloved church at Thyratira. When Jesus states that Jezebel "calleth herself a prophetess," He is saying that Jezebel isn't a prophetess at all; Jesus is also indicating that the church at Thyratira lacked the spiritual maturity to know the difference between a true seasoned prophet, the spirit of prophecy, and the office of prophet. In Thyatira, this spiritual immaturity became an open door for the seducing spirits of end times; thus, Jezebel was able to teach and seduce the Lord's servants to commit fornication. The believers joined themselves emotionally and spiritually to Jezebel, and became "charmed and unarmed." Rather than drinking from the Lord's fountain of living waters, the believers in Thyatira drank from an impure fountain that could not hold true sustenance, as we see in the book of Jeremiah.

Jeremiah 2:13 KJV
For my people have committed two evils; they have forsaken me the fountain of living waters, and hewed them out cisterns, broken cisterns, that can hold no water.

Beloved, the subtle seduction of the spirit of Jezebel happens in two ways: through the use of devious disguises, which we will explore in this chapter, and through the use of corrupt counsel, which we will examine in the next chapter.

Devious disguises are able to deceive us because we lack teaching from God's Word, as we see in the book of Hosea.

Hosea 4:6 KJV
My people are destroyed for lack of knowledge: because thou hast rejected knowledge, I will also reject thee, that thou shalt be no priest to me: seeing thou hast forgotten the law of thy God, I will also forget thy children.

The lack of discernment of the presence of evil spirits at work and the subsequent fallout of the faithful also comes from spiritual immaturity. This lack of discernment opens the door of deception to the trap of approaching spiritual death at the jaws of Jezebel. Unfortunately, there are self-appointed, self-anointed ministers that are not skilled enough in the Word, or that have not yet paid a price, that lead others astray by failing to teach them the pure, undefiled Word of God.

Beloved, we can be so deceived by what looks like the anointing and sounds like the anointing, but it is the spirit of Jezebel out to deceive God's very elect. Let's see what happened to Paul in the book of Acts.

Acts 16:16-18 KJV
[16] And it came to pass, as we went to prayer, a certain damsel possessed with a spirit of divination met us, which brought her masters much gain by soothsaying: [17] The same followed Paul and us,

and cried, saying, These men are the servants of the most high God, which shew unto us the way of salvation. [18] And this did she many days. But Paul, being grieved, turned and said to the spirit, I command thee in the name of Jesus Christ to come out of her. And he came out the same hour.

This young girl was possessed with a spirit of divination ("python" in Greek), but that evil spirit was not detected until Paul was grieved, meaning that the Holy Spirit in Paul was grieved. The spirit of divination contributed to friction in the flow of the anointing. Beloved, can you imagine being with Paul and experiencing a block in the anointing? This girl wore a devious disguise. It sounds so holy when she says, "These men are servants of the most High God," but there was nothing holy about what the girl was doing. The Bible says that she acted this way for many days, which means that it was difficult to immediately discern the presence of an evil spirit. Beloved, can you see that it looks like the anointing, it sounds like the anointing, but it's not the anointing? It is a carefully crafted attempt to seduce believers by sensationalism and deception; it is a devious disguise.

Another way that the spirit of Jezebel disguises things is by making good appear to be evil and evil appear to be good, as we see in the book of Matthew.

Matthew 12:22-24

[22] Then was brought unto him (Jesus) one possessed with a devil, blind, and dumb: and he healed him, insomuch that the blind and dumb both spake and saw. [23] And all the people were amazed, and said, Is not this the son of David? [24] But when the Pharisees heard it, they said, This fellow doth not cast out devils, but by Beelzebub the prince of the devils.

The spirit of Jezebel is also connected with witchcraft, or the tendency to cover things up, as we see in the book of 2 Kings.

2 Kings 9:22 KJV

And it came to pass, when Joram saw Jehu, that he said, Is it peace, Jehu? And he answered, What peace, so long as the whoredoms of thy mother Jezebel and her witchcrafts are so many?

The Hebrew word for witchcraft is "anan" which means to "cover up." When something is being "covered up," it looks like one thing, but it is really another thing. This means it is a devious disguise, which we can also see in the book of 2 Kings.

2 Kings 9:30 KJV

And when Jehu was come to Jezreel, Jezebel heard of it; and she painted her face, and tired her head, and looked out at a window.

The word "painted" is the word "soom" in Hebrew, which can also mean to disguise. Jezebel disguised her face because she didn't want Jehu to recognize her. Jezebel knew that Jehu had been anointed by

God to slay the house of Ahab and Jezebel, because they had killed the prophets of God.

The spirit of deceptive disguise connected with Jezebel was so strong that it also influenced Ahab; he was so manipulated that he eventually operated just like Jezebel. The Bible shows us how Ahab disguised himself when he went into battle so that he wouldn't be detected by the forces of an opposing army.

1 Kings 22:30 KJV
The King of Israel said unto Jehoshaphat, I will disguise myself, and enter into the battle; but put thou on thy robes. And the king of Israel disguised himself, and went into the battle.

Putting on a disguise is an indication that the enemy is warring against the people of God. Whenever there's something that's irritating the kingdom of darkness, whenever the people of God are winning territory for the Lord or are about to move forward into the next level of their destiny, the enemy puts on a disguise and fights against the people of God. Whenever we see disguises, whenever the enemy is trying to appear to be something else, we know that we are in a face-to-face confrontation with the spirit of Jezebel.

In order to identify and overcome deceptive disguises, we need to spend time alone with God and in His Word so that we always recognize His presence. We also need to continually test the spirits that come into our lives, as we see in the book of 1 John.

1 John 4:1 KJV
Beloved, believe not every spirit, but try the spirits whether they are of God: because many false prophets are gone out into the world.

Beloved readers, when we spend time with the Lord and follow His commandments, we will not be deceived by devious disguises. We will fulfill our destinies and be victorious, in the name of Jesus!

Prayer

Dear Lord,

I ask You to help me discern every deception from the spirit of Jezebel. I claim the full anointing of the Blood-bought victory that is mine through the cross and the resurrection. I ask You for keen discernment over any deception out to destroy my destiny. In the name of Jesus, amen!

Diary for Destiny

1. How would you define or describe the "deception of disguise" that the spirit of Jezebel uses?

2. Have you ever been influenced by a deceptive disguise? How did you handle the situation? Now that you have read this chapter, how might you have handled the situation more effectively?

Chapter 3

The Corrupt Counsel of Jezebel

Beloved, we are continuing our study of the spirit of Jezebel, including learning more about how this spirit operates and what we can do to obliterate this stronghold. In the last chapter, we learned about the first way that the spirit of Jezebel tries to negatively impact believers, which is to use deceptive disguises; in this chapter, we will focus on another way that the spirit of Jezebel tries to seduce believers, which is through corrupt counsel. The Bible tells us more about corrupt counsel in the book of 1 Kings.

1 Kings 21:25 KJV
But there was none like unto Ahab, which did sell himself to work wickedness in the sight of the LORD, whom Jezebel his wife stirred up.

Jezebel manipulated and stirred up Ahab through her corrupt counsel. The spirit of Jezebel often operates through corrupt counsel to deceive us out of our ministries and our destinies. Sometimes, beloved, the spirit of corrupt counsel will come to us when we are discouraged or when we are distracted by thinking about something like a pet peeve. This spirit subtly uses an array of emotional issues that sometimes succeed because we have not been taught how to be good soldiers of the cross. The jaws of Jezebel can easily seduce us out of our predestined purposes and positions if we have not been taught how to endure to the end. At some point in our lives, we will be tested on withstanding the wiles of Jezebel's witchcraft through the means of corrupt counsel.

We need to use discernment when we are making plans and decisions, and not be deceived by what we hear; sometimes the "counsel" that we hear from other people or even during our alone times can be offered in a deceptive manner. For example, Jezebel wasn't always demanding when she spoke with other people. Instead, sometimes she used a soft, flattering approach and would say things like, "Oh,

Ahab, you should have Naboth's vineyard. Aren't you the king? Just leave it in my hands. I'll get you the vineyard of Naboth" (see 1 Kings 21:7). The spirit of Jezebel will try to stir us up and play on our emotions. This spirit can even sound like our own voice and say things that our flesh would like to hear. This is why we need to take every thought into captivity and determine its source; otherwise, we might listen to and agree with thoughts from the enemy. Those thoughts can turn into strongholds and negatively influence our thinking and our actions. The enemy is strategic and knows the most effective time to inject evil thoughts into our lives; he will send thoughts that are contrary to the will of God when we are tired, offended, hurt, and weak. We must always carefully guard our thoughts and stay focused on the Word and will of God. We need to become experts in choosing which war we want to engage in: the war of God's design of destiny, or the war of the flesh that produces no profit. This is why offense must slide off of us like water off a duck's back. That can only happen through much prayer.

We can learn more about the characteristics of corrupt counsel by looking at the impact of the words of Athaliah, the daughter of Jezebel and Ahab.

2 Chronicles 22:2-3 KJV
[2] Forty and two years old was Ahaziah when he began to reign, and he reigned one year in Jerusalem. His mother's name also was Athaliah the (grand)daughter of Omri. [3] He also walked in the ways of the house of Ahab: for his mother was his counselor to do wickedly.

The spirit of Jezebel caused Athaliah to counsel her son to act wickedly and to reject the ways of the Lord. Wicked counsel influences us to stop serving God; it can also influence us to give up, to want to die, and to think that there is no reason for us to go on. There may be times when people give us bad advice, but that doesn't necessarily mean that they are being driven by evil; instead, they may be tired, or they might not have full understanding of a particular situation. But when someone gives us corrupt counsel with a demonic purpose, there's a bewitching that comes over our minds. Demonic counsel tries to make us want to die, to give up on our dreams, to make us feel unimportant, to make us feel like we're not worthy enough for God to use us, to make us feel burned out and desperate, and to make us feel like, "God, I never see any results." We start to think that we'll never make any progress, and that God doesn't really have a call on our lives, so we might as well just give up. That is a spirit of corrupt counsel, trying to discourage us and deceive us out of our destinies.

The spirit of corrupt counsel tries to not only disrupt the destinies of individuals, but also of entire nations. In the book of Ezra, we can see how the spirit of corrupt counsel tried to prevent the Israelites from rebuilding the temple and reestablishing worship of the Most High God in the land of Israel.

Ezra 4:1-5 KJV

[1] Now when the adversaries of Judah and Benjamin heard that the children of the captivity builded the temple unto the Lord God of Israel; [2] Then they came to Zerubbabel, and to the chief of the fathers, and said unto them, Let us build with you: for we seek God, as ye do; and we do sacrifice unto him since the days of Esar-haddon king of Assur, which brought us up hither. [3] But Zerubbabel, and Jeshua, and the rest of the chief of the fathers of Israel, said unto them, Ye have nothing to do with us to build an house unto our God; but we ourselves together will build unto the Lord God of Israel, as King Cyrus the king of Persia hath commanded us. [4] Then the people of the land weakened the hands of the people of Judah, and troubled them in building, [5] And hired counselors against them, to frustrate their purpose,

all the days of Cyrus king of Persia, even until the reign of Darius king of Persia.

In this passage, the text teaches that "(hiring) counselors against them to frustrate their purpose" means that it was a devious design to stop the rebuilding project by using the subliminal warfare of corrupt and crafty counsel. We can see that anytime we are moving in accordance with God's plan for our lives, anytime that we are making progress with our families, our businesses, or in any area of our lives, we will be opposed by spirits that don't want to see our success. These adversaries do not want us to take back territory or to rebuild the kingdom of God in any way. The enemy will try to send spirits on assignment or people on assignment to pull us away from the path that God has planned for us. The Hebrew word for "counselors," *ya'ats*, can also mean "conspirers." These evil spirits have already conspired a plot to pull us away from God's perfect plan for our lives, to make us lukewarm, to make us double-minded, to wear us out, and to frustrate us so that we give up on what God has called us to do.

In the book of 1 Kings, we see additional evidence of how powerful and demoralizing the spirit of corrupt counsel can be.

1 Kings 19:1-4 KJV
[1] And Ahab told Jezebel all that Elijah had done, and withal how he had slain all the prophets with the sword. [2] Then Jezebel send a messenger unto Elijah, saying, So let the gods do to me, and more also, if I make not thy life as the life of one of them by to morrow about this time. [3] And when he saw that, he arose, and went for his life, and came to Beersheba, which belongeth to Judah, and left his servant there. [4] But he himself went a day's journey into the wilderness, and came and sat down under a juniper tree: and he requested for himself that he might die; and said, It is enough; now, O Lord, take away my life; for I am not better than my fathers.

Elijah was a mighty man of God, but he was in a vulnerable state when he received the letter from Jezebel. He had just brought down 450 prophets of Baal and 400 priests of Asherah, and his servant didn't really know how to protect the man of God and the anointing on Elijah's life. Elijah was vulnerable because his armorbearer (his servant) had not grown into the place of power needed to support Elijah's calling, as we see in the following verses:

1 Kings 18:43-44 KJV
[43] And said to his servant, Go up now, look toward the sea. And he went up, and looked, and said, There is nothing. And he said, Go again seven times. [44] And it came to pass at the seventh time, that he said, Behold, there ariseth a little cloud out of the sea, like a man's hand. And he said, Go up, say unto Ahab, Prepare thy chariot, and get thee down that the rain stop thee not.

1 Kings 19:3b KJV

He (Elijah) came to Beersheba, which belongeth to Judah, and left his servant there.

When we read that Elijah "left his servant there," this means that the armor bearer was not equipped to protect the man of God in his battle against strongholds. As a result, Elijah fled for his life. Now Elijah is forced by the spirit of Jezebel out of the region of his ministry because Elijah was a prophet to the northern kingdom of Israel. So when Elijah read the letter from Jezebel cursing him and pronouncing words of death, Elijah wanted to perish. The strength of these words coming against Elijah was so strong that the Bible says "he sat down under a juniper tree and requested that he might die" (1 Kings 19:4). These were words so diabolical that they intended to block him from returning to the northern kingdom. The terror tactic of Jezebel was to use the witchcraft of words as a form of intimidation, manipulation, and control. As we have seen earlier, the spirit of corrupt counsel strikes when we are in a weak or vulnerable position, and the results can be devastating.

But if we remain faithful in the fight against the spirits that are trying to move us out of our place or ministry, God will reward us with an increase in the anointing. We see this happen in the life of Elijah, as he became able to hear God in a still, small voice (1 Kings 9:12).

Beloved, what more can we do to overcome the spirit of Jezebel?

First of all, we can see that God prefigures the power of prayer and fasting as a supernatural solution to conquer the spirit of Jezebel in the book of 1 Kings.

1 Kings 19:6-8 KJV
[6] And he looked, and, behold, there was a cake baken on the coals, and a cruse of water at his head. And he did eat and drink, and laid him down again. [7] And the angel of the Lord came again the second time, and touched him, and said, Arise and

eat; because the journey is too great for thee. [8] And he arose, and did eat and drink, and went in the strength of that meat forty days and forty nights unto Horeb the mount of God.

The text teaches that "he went in the strength of that meat 40 days and nights unto Horeb the mount of God." The "strength of that meat" means the gift of grace that God will give us as we apply the weapons of war of fasting and prayer against the spirit of Jezebel.

We can see further evidence of the importance of prayer and fasting in the story of Obadiah and the prophets as a strategy to overcome the spirit of Jezebel in the book of 1 Kings.

1 Kings 18:3-4 KJV
[3] And Ahab called Obadiah, which was the governor of his house. Now Obadiah feared the Lord greatly: [4] For it was so, when Jezebel cut off the prophets of the Lord, that Obadiah took an

hundred prophets, and hid them by fifty in a cave, and fed them with bread and water.

God had strategically planted Obadiah in the house of Ahab, and Obadiah understood that he was part of the king's household for a divine purpose. When Ahab and Jezebel were planning to kill the prophets of Israel, Obadiah heard about the evil plot because he was part of the household. Obadiah knew that he needed to do something about the situation. He risked his life and hid the prophets in a cave, and fed them with bread and water. Hiding in a cave represents having prayer time alone with God, while bread and water represent fasting and prayer. When there is a serious situation in our own lives or in the lives of others that involves a spirit of Jezebel, we need to spend prayer time alone with God and earnestly seek His solution. We cannot fight spiritual powers with the flesh; we need to seek the Lord's war strategy to conquer a spirit like Jezebel. As 2 Corinthians 10:3-5 KJV states, "For though we walk in the flesh, we do not war after the flesh: (for the weapons of our warfare are not carnal, but mighty through God to the pulling down of strong holds;) casting down imaginations, and every high thing that exalteth itself against the knowledge of God, and bringing into captivity every thought to the obedience of Christ."

Secondly, we need to commit to fighting against a spirit of Jezebel until we have achieved victory. A battle that goes on for a long time is called wrestling, and fighting a spirit of Jezebel is usually a wrestling match. Wrestling doesn't involve little demons; if we've been fighting a spiritual battle more than a week or two, then that's an indication that we're wrestling against principalities, against a demonic prince that is out to destroy our families and our lives. We can't give up overnight; we have to stay in the battle, stay in the fight. We need to use different types of warfare weapons, like fasting and prayer. We have to use longevity of prayer and faithfulness, and declare everyday that, "I believe that God will bring the victory, and I will not waver in my faith; I know that I already have the things that the Word has promised, and in the name of Jesus, I am not going to stop until the spirit of Jezebel is obliterated." If we don't feel a release in the Spirit, we need to stay in the battle until the spirit of Jezebel is brought down.

We can find a third strategy for conquering the spirit of Jezebel in the life of Elijah in the book of 1 Kings.

1 Kings 18:30 KJV
And Elijah said unto all the people, Come near unto me. And all the people came near unto him. And he repaired the altar of the Lord that was broken down.

We need to look at our lives and see if there are any ways that the altar of the Lord has broken down. Is our sacrifice and service to the Lord in need of repair? Are we serving Him wholeheartedly and with passion? Are there any areas of compromise in our lives? Are we still working on the assignments that

He has given us to do, in the places where He has called us to serve? We need to be faithful and complete our God-given assignments; God will always give us the grace to complete the tasks He has assigned to us. We must examine our lives and make sure that the altar of the Lord, our sacrifice and service to Him, are in a state of excellence.

Beloved people of God, now that we have a clearer understanding of how the spirit of Jezebel operates, we must obliterate this evil stronghold, in the mighty name of Jesus!

I want to conclude this chapter with a personal word of encouragement for you: I believe right now that you are being anointed for the supernatural strategy and gift of grace to bring down every assignment against your destiny. I believe as you ask God for the grace to fight this battle that He will give you a strategy of power so that you will not only win the battle, but you will also bring out of the battle a greater anointing, increased ministry, greater wisdom, and a double portion destiny.

Psalm 66:12b KJV

We went through fire and through water: but Thou broughtest us out into a wealthy place.

Prayer

Dear Lord,

I ask You to help me to interpret every situation in my life from Your perspective. I declare and decree that I will not be influenced by any corrupt counsel. Give me strength and discernment so that I will not be pulled away from my calling under any conditions. In the name of Jesus, amen!

Diary for Destiny

1. How would you describe what "corrupt counsel" is?

2. Has there ever been a situation in your life when you were given "corrupt counsel"? How did you handle the situation? Now that you have read this chapter, how might you have handled the situation more effectively?

Chapter 4

The Seducing Spirit of Delilah

Beloved, in the last days, there will be evil spirits assigned to remove the anointing from our lives and to deceive us out of our destinies. One of these deceptive entities is the spirit of Delilah. In this chapter, we will learn more about the serpentine nature of the spirit of Delilah; in the next chapter, we will learn about how this serpentine spirit tried to derail Samson's destiny, and how we can prevent this spirit from affecting our lives.

In the book of Judges, the story of Samson and Delilah is a prophetic prefiguring in documented detail of how this spirit operates. I believe the author of the book of Judges, the prophet Samuel, has a prophetic insight for every generation that exceeds a narrative of Hebrew history. The mission of the prophets leaves a legacy of teaching to every generation that is personal, powerful, prophetic, and relevant. The writings of the prophets in scripture are timeless in terms of their prophetic agenda and intent.

We will begin our study of the spirit of Delilah by looking at scripture passages from 1 Timothy 4 and Judges 16.

1 Timothy 4:1-2 KJV

[1] Now the Spirit speaketh expressly, that in the latter times some shall depart from the faith, giving heed to seducing spirits, and doctrines of devils; [2] Speaking lies in hypocrisy; having their conscience seared with a hot iron.

Judges 16:4-6 KJV

[4] And it came to pass afterward, that he (Samson) loved a woman in the valley of Sorek, whose name was Delilah. [5] And the lords of the Philistines came up unto her, and said unto her, Entice him, and see wherein his great strength lieth, and by what means we may prevail against him, that we may bind him to afflict him: and we will give thee every one of us eleven hundred pieces of silver. [6]

And Delilah said to Samson, Tell me, I pray thee, wherein thy great strength lieth, and wherewith thou mightest be bound to afflict thee.

Judges 16:17-20 KJV

[17] That he told her all his heart, and said unto her, There hath not come a razor upon mine head; for I have been a Nazarite unto God from my mother's womb: if I be shaven, then my strength will go from me, and I shall become weak, and be like any other man. [18] And when Delilah saw that he told her all his heart, she sent and called for the lords of the Philistines, saying, Come up this once, for he hath shewed me all his heart. Then the lords of the Philistines came up unto her, and brought money in their hand. [19] And she made him sleep upon her knees; and she called for a man, and she caused him to shave off the seven locks of his head; and she began to afflict him, and his strength went from him. [20] And she said, The Philistines be upon thee, Samson. And he awoke out of his sleep, and said, I will go out as at other times before, and

shake myself. And he wist not that the Lord was departed from him.

The seducing spirits mentioned in these passages, including the spirit of Delilah, are strong endtime forces, but the bondage breaking power of God can and will deliver us! Throughout the Bible, we see that God provides His protection to prevent us from being deceived by these endtime spirits, through knowledge of His Word and the Holy Spirit.

However, it is important that we do our part and have an understanding of how these evil spirits work. 1 Timothy 4:1 tells us that some people will give heed to seducing spirits in the last days. In a Greek sense of scripture, "giving heed" also means to give one's mind over to something or to give oneself entirely over to something. "Giving heed" comes from the Greek word "prosechontes," which means to focus. "Giving heed" in this sense means that our entire attention is concentrated on something; for example, if we are painting a room, we put all our attention and all our strength into the activity, and we ignore any distractions that come along in order to do a great job. But "prosechontes" can also work in a negative sense; if we don't have an understanding about how spirits work, then a spirit can come and take hold of our minds (prosechontes) through seducing subtleties without our even realizing what has happened.

The operation and manipulation of evil spirits is often a slow, seducing process. We need to realize that spirits don't just jump on us and then have control over us; we have to give them permission to enter in some way. Remember this: no admission without permission! In Luke 8:32, the text teaches that the spirits in the demoniac of the Gaderenes asked for permission to enter the swine as Jesus cast them out: scripture says that "Jesus suffered them," which meant that he gave them permission. Oftentimes spirits will try to affect us by first influencing our thinking. This is why we must gird up the loins of our mind (1 Peter 1:13). Some people are spiritually strong and take authority over thoughts from the enemy immediately, saying, "I bind you in the name of Jesus – get out of here!" or "I rebuke that carnal, un-Christlike thought or wicked imagination!" These spiritually perceptive people vanquish those thoughts from the enemy right away and put them under the blood of Jesus. But some of us are weak-minded. If a thought from the enemy comes into our minds, we think about that thought all day long, and soon our whole being can be consumed by that thought. Once we entertain thoughts from the enemy in our minds, those thoughts can lead to changes in our attitude, then our decisions begin to change, and then our destiny begins to change. Subtly we have been seduced into a wrong attitude. Subtly that seduction pulls us out of our place. Subtly we are seduced into a change of attitude toward a person that we have been called to support or a ministry that God has given us to serve in.

The apostle Paul refers to these spirits as "seducing spirits," because this means that they are spirits that are serpentine in nature. We can learn more about serpentine spirits through studying the book of Genesis.

Genesis 3:1 KJV
Now the serpent was more subtle than any beast of the field which the Lord God had made. And he said unto the woman, Yea, hath God said, Ye shall not eat of every tree of the garden?

In scripture, the word "beast" doesn't always refer to the animal kingdom: "beast" can also be used to refer to spirits. So when we are talking about serpentine spirits, we don't necessarily mean literal creatures crawling on the ground. From the scripture we can see that the word "beasts" refers to the demonic spirits that Jesus encountered in the wilderness, as described in the book of Mark.

Mark 1:13 KJV

And He was there in the wilderness forty days, tempted of Satan and was with the wild beasts: and the angels of God there ministered unto Him.

During the time that Jesus was fasting for 40 days and 40 nights in the wilderness, He encountered "wild beasts." The Greek word translated as "wild beasts" is "therion," which is spiritually synonymous with the demonic powers that Jesus broke in the wilderness through His prayer and fasting.

These demonic powers or serpentine spirits will try to deceive us out of our destiny, and try to lead us away from God's plan for our lives by influencing us with deceiving thoughts, like tempting us to be angry about certain situations or people. These deceiving spirits are on assignment to make us see our situations in the flesh. This is why demonic influences have free reign over the mind of Christians who consistently neglect to take responsibility for their thoughts or who are unable to manage their emotions.

Romans 8:7 KJV
Because the carnal mind is enmity against God: for it is not subject to the law of God, neither indeed can be.

Believers need to know how to put their flesh under the subjection of the Holy Spirit; otherwise we have a church that enters into deception fairly easily. We need to learn how to prefer others before ourselves; as Philippians 2:3-4 states, "Let nothing be done through strife or vainglory; but in lowliness of mind let each esteem other better than themselves. Look not every man on his own things, but every man also on the things of others."

We find further descriptions of serpentine spirits in the following verses:

2 Corinthians 11:3 KJV
But I fear, lest by any means, as the serpent beguiled Eve through his subtility, so your minds should be corrupted from the simplicity that is in Christ.

Revelations 12:9a KJV
And the great dragon was cast out, that old serpent, called the Devil, and Satan, which deceiveth the whole world.

As believers, our destiny is to overcome and to take up serpentine spirits. These are spirits that primarily influence our minds and prey on our emotions and weaknesses. These are spirits that can eventually claim ownership over areas of our mind that continually give them entrance. This is why we must always take into captivity every thought and cause it to be Christ-like, pure, noncritical, kind, ready to serve, not boastful, and surrendered to God's will. Let's look at what Jesus says about our authority over serpentine spirits in the book of Mark.

Mark 16:17-18 KJV

[17] And these signs shall follow them that believe; In my name shall they cast out devils; they shall speak with new tongues; [18] They shall take up serpents; and if they drink any deadly thing, it shall not hurt them; they shall lay hands on the sick, and they shall recover.

"Taking up serpents" is a reference to the way that God demonstrated His power and authority over evil spirits through Moses as the Israelites were getting ready to break free from the bondage of Egypt. Let's look at the book of Exodus. In Exodus 4:2-4, the text teaches the supernatural significance of why the rod of Moses became a serpent and turned back into a rod again.

Exodus 4:2-4 KJV

[2] And the Lord said unto him: What is that in thine hand? And he said, A rod. [3] And He said, Cast it on the ground, And he cast it on the ground, and it became a serpent; and Moses fled from

before it. [4] And the Lord said unto Moses, Put forth thine hand, and take it by the tail. And he put forth his hand, and caught it, and it became a rod in his hand.

According to Midrashic rabbinic sources, cultic priests in ancient Egypt used to charm snakes and cause them to become calm and passive. They would do this through pressing on a certain nerve in a snake's neck and it would become stiff like a rod. In the passage above, God tells Moses to throw his rod down, and it became a snake; then God told Moses to take up the snake by its tail, and it became a rod again in his hand. When Moses took the snake by the tail and it turned into a rod, this was a genuine miracle occurring; the snake wasn't simply becoming stiff because a nerve in the back of its neck was being pressed, as was the case with the snakes of the cultic priests.

Moreover, the rod represents the anointing of God. All of the signs and wonders in Egypt, including the plagues and the parting of the Red Sea, happened through the rod of Moses and the rod of Aaron. The rod also represents the superiority and authority of the anointing over evil spirits. We see in Exodus 7 how Moses' and Aaron's rod swallows up the rods of the Egyptian priests. God further demonstrates the authority and superiority of His anointing in Exodus 12:12, when He said, "For I will pass through the land of Egypt this night, and will smite the firstborn in the land of Egypt, both man and beast; and against all the gods of Egypt I will execute judgment: I am the LORD." Executing judgment against the gods of Egypt meant that God was going to execute judgment against the spirits that controlled Egypt and against the serpentine wicked spirits that had kept the people of God in bondage for 400 years. Those spirits had to be dealt with before the people of God could come out of bondage. The same principle holds true today; sometimes there are spirits that have to be dealt with before we break out of bondage, before we get to the next level, and before we come forth to the new place that the Lord has planned for us.

Prayer

Dear Lord,

I give you praise and I give You thanks. Help me to keep my mind always focused on You. Help me to bring every thought into obedience, and show me how to walk in the spiritual authority that You have given me. To You be the glory! In Jesus' name, amen!

Diary for Destiny

1. Have you ever spent a lot of time thinking a thought that wasn't from the Lord? Can you see any patterns with respect to how the enemy started to affect your thoughts (e.g. through anger, depression, jealousy, etc.)?

2. Whenever the enemy tries to influence your thoughts in the future, what steps will you take to make sure that your thoughts stay focused on things that are true, right, noble, pure, and lovely (Philippians 4:8)?

Chapter 5

Deliverance from the Deception of Delilah

In the previous chapter, we examined the serpentine nature of the spirit of Delilah; in this chapter, we will learn more about the specific challenges that Samson faced and the importance of remaining on fire for God and maintaining our consecration to the Lord.

Beloved readers, you may remember that the calling on Samson's life was to break Israel out of spiritual bondage and to deliver Israel out of the hand of the Philistines. The 40-year-long captivity of Israel under the Philistines was the longest, strongest bondage that the Israelites had experienced since they had left Egypt. The bondage was particularly strong in the sense that the Philistines had so subdued the Israelites that the children of God didn't want to cause any kind of conflict with the Philistines; there was a national sense of apathy among the Israelites. They did not want confrontation and they lived without liberation. But God only needed one person to break the bondage of the Philistines, and He was preparing Samson to be that leader, just as I believe you are being prepared to be that leader *today*.

Samson's consecration, or Nazarite vow, was a primary key that prepared him to free Israel from the bondage of the Philistines. This consecration began even before Samson was born, as we see in the passage below when the angel of the Lord talked with Samson's mother. The vow of consecration was the secret of his strength. God needed supernatural consecration in an apathetic generation.

Judges 13:4-5 KJV
[4] Now therefore beware, I pray thee, and drink not wine nor strong drink, and eat not any unclean thing: [5] For lo, thou shalt conceive, and bear a son; and no razor shall come on his head: for the child shall be a Nazarite unto God from the womb:

and he shall begin to deliver Israel out of the hand of the Philistines.

A Nazarite vow during that period in Israel's history typically lasted around 30 days. People who had taken a Nazarite vow didn't cut the locks of their hair or the hair growing on the sides of their faces; they also didn't touch or consume grapes and wine. During the time that Samson lived, wine was a primary drink of individuals who lived in Israel, so avoiding grapes and wine was a challenging task. A Nazarite vow was a strong vow of consecration, and people who made the vow were considered to be separated unto God during the length of the vow. In some circumstances, people made lifelong Nazarite vows and the consecration lasted their entire lives. Because the angel of the Lord told Samson's mother that her son was to be a Nazarite unto God from the womb, Samson's mother observed a Nazarite vow the entire time that she was pregnant with Samson. And Samson himself was supposed to be consecrated as a Nazarite for his entire lifetime.

Some others in scripture who had lifelong Nazarite vows were the prophet Samuel (1 Samuel 1:11) and John the Baptist (Luke 1:15).

However, Samson faced some particular circumstances that made it difficult to keep a Nazarite vow for his entire lifetime. Samson probably had to walk a solitary walk more than almost any other person in the Bible. Everyone in the Bible who is really used of God had to walk a solitary walk, but Samson was especially misunderstood by his generation. Other people didn't understand his consecration, and they didn't understand his walk with God. Samson continually engaged in individual conflicts with the Philistines, as he was led by the Lord; Samson would have a relationship with someone and cause a confrontation with that person, for the justice of the Lord. But most people in Samson's life didn't understand how God was using him to break Israel free from the bondage of the Philistines; in Judges 15, we even see that Samson's own countrymen turned him over to the

Philistines because they felt that he was causing confrontation with the Philistines. The Bible also says that Samson's own father and mother didn't understand that Samson's marriage with his first Philistine wife was of the Lord. In Judges 14:4, the text teaches that "his father and his mother knew not that it was of the LORD, that he sought an occasion against the Philistines."

Samson experienced great success in his battles with the Philistines, but there came a time in his life that he grew tired and let his guard down. The rabbis teach that Samson was most likely in his 60s when he fell in love with Delilah. When Delilah entered the picture, Samson fell in love with her. Delilah was able to influence him because he didn't have resistance and his level of consecration had already begun to diminish through the inability to recover himself after retaliation from the enemy for so many victories for God. He allowed discouragement to enter in, and he allowed himself to be taken away from his place of fervency and service to God. He became so accustomed to the presence of God that his service to the Lord became mechanical.

Beloved, it is our personal responsibility to remain on fire for God. If we see that our prayer lives are lacking, we better do something about it. We shouldn't wait for trials that knock us down, knock us out, or to come our way. God did not make those trials happen; instead they happened because we opened a door. We were not in our watchtower watching for God, we got out of the Spirit by laxity, and we allowed ourselves to get into a bad place that threw us off. Let us take back the territory of our intimate fellowship and communion with Him. Let us regain the taken territory by appropriating the grace of God that will cause us to do the impossible! Let's seek God because we love Him with all our heart, our soul, our mind, and our strength, and we cannot live without Him.

Scripture documents the details of how Samson's struggle was a misunderstood sign of consecration in an apathetic generation.

Judges 15:9-10 KJV
[9] Then the Philistines went up, and pitched in Judah, and spread themselves in Lehi. [10] And the men of Judah said, Why are ye come up against us? And they answered, To bind Samson are we come up, to do to him as he hath done to us.

Let's take a closer look at what's happening here. The men of Judah have noticed that the Philistines have invaded their territory, and are asking, "Why have you come? What did we do to stir you up? We thought we were paying taxes, and that we were doing everything that you wanted us to do. We thought we had an agreement that if we submitted ourselves to you, you were not going to come and bother us." But that attitude was an indication of a bigger problem. Notice that the Israelites didn't tell the Philistines to get out of their land and that they didn't try to fight the Philistines. The Israelites were basically trying to appease the Philistines and keep them appeased. The Philistines replied that they had come to bind Samson; they intended to do to Samson what Samson had done to them (a retaliatory tactic).

This is what happens when there's a major spiritual victory for God's kingdom: retaliation. Sometimes when there's territory taken for the kingdom of God, the enemy knows what's happening, and tries to come back at us for what we did to his kingdom. But in the name of Jesus, we rebuke that spirit of retaliation! The spirit of God is on us and we cannot be bound.

We need intercessors to cover the work of God and His children in prayer. Intercessors have a responsibility to prevent retaliation from happening; they need to be at their posts ready to protect the work of God, especially when damage is done to the kingdom of darkness.

Judges 15:11-15 KJV

[11] Then three thousand men of Judah went to the top of the rock Etam, and said to Samson, Knowest thou not that the Philistines are rulers over us? What is this that thou has done unto us? And he said unto them, As they did unto me, so I have done unto them. [12] And they said unto him, We are come down to bind thee, that we may deliver thee into the hand of the Philistines. And Samson said unto them, Swear unto me, that ye will not fall upon me yourselves. [13] And they spake unto him, saying, No; but we will bind thee fast, and deliver thee into their hand: but surely we will not kill thee. And they bound him with two new cords, and brought him up from the rock. [14] And when he came unto Lehi, the Philistines shouted against him: and the Spirit of the Lord came mightily upon him, and the cords that were upon his arms became as flax that was burnt with fire and his bands loosed from off his hands. [15] And he found a new jawbone of a donkey, and put forth his hand, and took it, and slew a thousand men therewith.

Samson was so close to God; he wasn't worried when his fellow Israelites came to turn him over to the Philistines, because he knew that the power of God would be with him in a mighty way. Samson was a consecrated man in the middle of an apathetic generation, and God used him mightily – until Samson let his guard down. He was accustomed to being isolated and separated for his great calling to deliver Israel out of the hand of the Philistines after 40 years of domination.

What does it mean to let "one's guard down?" The Bible tells us about the importance of consistency and perseverance in the book of Matthew.

Matthew 24:12-13 KJV
[2] And because iniquity shall abound, the love of many shall wax cold. [3] But he that shall endure unto the end, the same shall be saved.

Once we have achieved victory in a certain battle, we need to stay on task and on guard until God has released us from our assignment. But Samson let his guard down after achieving a victory over the Philistines, and Delilah came into his life, during a time when he was also weary from the betrayal of his countrymen.

The name Delilah means "to weaken, or to make weak" in Hebrew. This name accurately describes the work that Delilah did in Samson's life. We need to know that the author of the book of Judges, the prophet Samuel, often changed the real names of individuals and gave them fictitious names that described their characters or something about the circumstances of their lives. Delilah's real name was probably not Delilah, but the prophet Samuel called her Delilah because it described her work in Samson's life. Delilah was on assignment to weaken Samson and to bring him down; her mission was to take the supernatural secret of strength out of Samson's life. The deception of Delilah aims to take the secret of our strength out of our lives and pull us out of our place. This spirit tries to make ministry mechanical, so that we walk the walk and talk the talk, but without any passion or anointing. It is a spirit that seduces us to surrender the secret of who we have been called to be and what we have been called to do.

The spirit of Delilah tries to secularize the supernatural aspects of our lives and persistently attempts to remove the anointing from our lives. This is because the anointing is strength (Isaiah 10:27).

In a hermeneutical sense of scripture, we see the phrases "Tell me how you might be bound" and "I shall be weak as another man" multiple times, which indicates that these are primary principles in the text. The spirit of Delilah wants to steal the anointing and seduce believers into surrendering the secret of their strength; this spirit persistently says, "Give your strength to me."

Judges 16:6-7 KJV

[6] And Delilah said to Samson, Tell me, I pray thee, wherein thy great strength lieth, and wherewith thou mightest be bound to afflict thee. [7] And Samson said unto her, If they bind me with seven green withs that were never dried, then shall I be weak and be as another man.

Judges 16:10-11 KJV

[10] And Delilah said unto Samson, Behold, thou hast mocked me, and told me lies: now tell me, I pray thee, wherewith thou mightest be bound. [11] And he said unto her, If they bind me fast with new ropes that never were occupied, then shall I be weak, and be as another man.

Judges 6:13 KJV

And Delilah said unto Samson, Hitherto thou hast mocked me, and told me lies: tell me wherewith thou mightest be bound. And he said unto her, If thou weavest the seven locks of my head with the web.

In the following passages we see how Delilah seduced Samson into apathy, symbolized by Samson sleeping on her knees, and then was able to steal his strength. Shaving off the seven locks of hair means that she stole the sign of his consecration. She stole his Nazarite vow. She began to afflict him and he had no power left. Remember: we will have no power in this generation if we lose our consecration.

Judges 16:15-17 KJV
[15] And she said unto him, How canst thou say, I love thee, when thine heart is not with me? thou hast mocked me these three times, and hast not told me wherein thy great strength lieth. [16] And it came to pass, when she pressed him daily with her words, and urged him, so that his soul was vexed unto death; [17] That he told her all his heart, and said unto her, There hath not come a razor upon mine head; for I have been a Nazarite unto God from my mother's womb: if I be shaven, then my strength will go from me, and I shall become weak, and be like any other man.

Judges 16:19 KJV

And she made him [Samson] sleep upon her knees; and she called for a man, and she caused him to shave off the seven locks of his head; and she began to afflict him, and his strength went from him.

We see the words "bound" and "afflict" used multiple times throughout the chapter of Judges 16. The word "bound" is the word "asar" in Hebrew, which also means to put a yoke on; and the word "afflict" is the word "ana" in Hebrew, which means to bow down or to look down upon. Delilah was aiming to put a yoke and bondage on Samson so that he couldn't go any further in God, that he would stay stuck in a state of apathy for the rest of his life. Once Samson's consecration of the Nazarite vow had ended, as indicated by the cutting of his hair, he would be weak, like any other individual without the anointing. In contrast, the anointing turns us into another person far beyond our natural capacity.

1 Samuel 10:6 KJV
And the Spirit of the Lord will come upon thee, and thou shalt prophesy with them, and shalt be turned into another man.

Delilah wanted to get Samson to a place where she could lower the level of his destiny and lower the level of who he was as a person. Once the enemy can influence us to stop our consecration and takes away our anointing, we are secularized; we have been brought down to a natural level. Without the anointing, we go down to a lower level. With the anointing, we come up to a higher level; through the anointing we reach the supernatural summit and peak of God's power in our lives.

Sometimes it seems that believers have spiritual amnesia and we forget what life was like without the anointing. We forget about the rejection, the abuse, and the way that people used to view us, because once the anointing came into our lives, God gave us purpose. We were given a place, we were given a position, and we were given a calling.

Prayer

Dear Lord,

Help me see the "secret" of my strength. I want to know the secret of my calling and how it works. I know I am not a carbon copy of someone else. You have given me a unique calling. Please show me the "secret" of the uniqueness of this call for my highest dimension of destiny. Help me discern the deception of Delilah. Give me the strength to never surrender the vision or the purpose of the high calling of God in Christ. In the name of Jesus, amen!

Diary for Destiny

1. Have you ever made "rollercoaster" decisions? For example, have you ever said "yes" to God concerning a mandate or mission, no matter how large or small, and then let circumstances or your emotions push you into changing your decision?

2. If you changed your mind about a commitment that you had made to God, can you truly face yourself and say, "I was too tired and couldn't pay the price"? Are you willing to receive the grace and anointing abundantly available to pursue your purpose?

3. What unique gift has God given you to contribute to this generation?

4. How is the spirit of Delilah trying to deceive you out of your destiny? What steps will you take to overcome this spirit that is trying to deceive you?

Chapter 6

Disobedience and Deficits to Destiny

Beloved readers, by now you may be asking yourselves the following questions: How do I discern God's voice? What if I think God is telling me something that I don't want to hear?

I remember hearing a sermon from Kathryn Kuhlman when I was a young girl in 1974, two years before she went home to be with the Lord. She approached the pulpit at Melodyland Christian Center in her long, beautiful, flowing dress, with fire in her eyes, and held a letter in her hand. We all fastened our eyes on the letter. It was quite unusual for Miss Kuhlman to begin a sermon with reading a letter. As she lifted the letter, she said, "I just received this letter from my dear friend, Garth Hunt." She continued to tell us about the valiant obedience of this young missionary who was challenged to do

God's will under the most life threatening conditions. She also spoke of the missionaries in his compound who at that time had been recently martyred, familiarizing us with the story of their slaughter on the streets of Saigon.

Young ministers and missionaries meant so much to Kathryn Kuhlman. The end of her life was filled with the quest of leading them into the place of great power and intimacy with the Holy Spirit. With tears rolling down her face, she told us how Garth had attended her miracle service at Shrine Auditorium and then had met her in the lobby of the Central Plaza Hotel, seeking her advice on how to discern God's voice for his difficult decision about whether or not to return to Saigon. As she described the incredibly difficult choice that Garth was facing, she made it clear that if he would choose to return, the choice could require the loss of his life. The letter she read contained in it details about the Thompsons, the missionary colleagues who made national headlines as they were slaughtered by the

Viet Cong for preaching the gospel. Now Garth desperately wanted to know what to do and was thrashing the thought in his mind, "Do I return and risk my life?"

The answer Miss Kuhlman gave was this: "I cannot tell you the will of God, but to miss God's will would be hell. And if I were you, before I would compromise, I would go."

The letter in her hand was from Garth on his way to the destination that was so difficult a choice to make. Kathryn's words resound in my mind and heart: "There goes the saint of God."

What did Miss Kuhlman mean, when she said that "to miss God's will would be hell"? It reminds me of one of God's chosen servants, His anointed prophet Jonah, who refused to do God's will and found himself in the darkness, isolation, and separation of the belly of the whale.

Jonah was not a false prophet by any means, but Jonah was a foolish prophet. There is a clear, concise difference between a false prophet and a foolish prophet. False prophets are those who masquerade as true prophets, and are dangerously influenced by the spirit of Jezebel. Foolish prophets are those who have an incredible call of God, but have fallen to a "lower level" outside their highest potential because they did not appropriate the available grace to do what was difficult and repugnant to their will.

What message is Jonah leaving with every generation about his decision? What is the secret his incredible message gives to us on the pages of scripture?

The story of Jonah tells us that to get out of God's will is to "flee from the presence of the Lord." We see this phrase appear twice in Jonah 1:3.

Jonah 1:3 KJV
But Jonah rose up to flee unto Tarshish from the presence of the Lord, and went down to Joppa; and he found a ship going to Tarshish: so he paid the fare thereof, and went down into it, to go with them unto Tarshish from the presence of the Lord.

Beloved, this means that the author's intent is to show us that disobeying the word of the Lord is the same thing as fleeing from the presence of the Lord. Jesus used the teaching about the prophet Jonah as a sign to a wicked and adulterous generation.

Matthew 12:39 KJV
But He answered and said unto them, An evil and adulterous generation seeketh after a sign; and there shall no sign shall be given to it, but the sign of the prophet Jonah.

Mathew 16:4a KJV
A wicked and adulterous generation seeketh after a

sign; and there shall be no sign given unto it, but the sign of the prophet Jonah.

The prophet Jonah provides a prophetic parallel of what will be happening in the last days. Jonah represents those in the last days who will fall away from their calling and will not walk in the highest dimension of their destiny. Jonah is a sign of a generation that wants to be used by God, but has blatantly refused to do ministry and to serve God in the way that He has asked. These people refuse to do what God has asked them to do because it's something that they find repugnant; it's something that they don't want to do.

Oftentimes the Lord will ask us to do things that we don't want to do. We may need to be with people we don't want to be with, love people we don't want to love, forgive people we don't want to forgive, help people we don't want to help, or go places we don't want to go. We can find all kinds of reasons not to do what God is asking us to do: it's too tiring, we're too weary, it's too taxing on the body, it's too inconvenient, or it costs too much. It's repugnant, and we resist the repugnant. That was the attitude of the prophet Jonah.

There is a tendency in the body of believers to think that something is God's will when it makes us feel comfortable, and when it allows us to be with people that we like, who we get along with, and who understand us. If something will cause our flesh to die, will cause us not to be seen of men, and may require the anointing of supernatural sacrifice, we may think that it's not God's will. When we think like that, we've become like Jonah. Jonah was a foolish prophet – not a false prophet, but a foolish prophet – who became a sign to show us that those who go in the wrong direction and refuse to pay the price of destiny can experience a severe alteration in the divine destination of destiny.

In order to understand what's happening in the book of Jonah, we need to understand the cross. The cross is the power of God and salvation; the cross also represents doing something that goes against our will. If God asks us to do something and if we are being influenced by corrupt counsel that tells us that we can't do it, we're not strong enough, we don't have the money, or we're going to be lonely, then we are being deceived. Through the cross, we have dominion over demonic principalities and powers!

Historically speaking, there is a little more than meets the eye in Jonah's story. The Midrash, which is a series of commentaries written by rabbis hundreds of years ago, tells us more about who Jonah is. I consider Midrash to be a reliable source of accurate, historical documentation. First of all, the Midrash tells us that Jonah is the son of the widow at Zarephath. Jonah had been raised from the dead; it was his destiny to die and be raised from the dead. Elijah the prophet had stretched over his body three times and raised him from the dead. Elijah was Jonah's spiritual father and Elisha was Jonah's teacher. There's no prophet like Elijah, and Elisha was the greatest miracle worker in the Hebrew scriptures. Also, Jonah's mother was the one who had given her last meal to the prophet Elijah and had seen the miraculous multiplication of grain that sustained her and her family through the rest of the famine. Jonah was raised by a mother who walked by faith and not by sight, who taught him obedience from the time he was a child, and who saved his life in a famine through her obedience. Jonah had an amazing spiritual pedigree.

So how did Jonah end up in the belly of a whale? What does it mean? Is there a personal, powerful, prophetic message for us today? Jonah lost the anointing through his disobedience, when he fled from the presence of the Lord. Jonah didn't want to do what God had told him and refused to testify to the Ninevites. Jonah wasn't obedient and he lost the anointing on his life. When we lose the anointing, we go back to where we would have been without the anointing. Jonah had died when he was a boy, and had been redeemed to serve the Lord. Being raised from the dead is a prophetic parallel of a born again experience; it is a prophetic parallel of why we have been redeemed. If we walk away from the purpose of why we have been redeemed, the anointing leaves our lives. Jonah would have been in the grave if he had not been raised for the purposes of God, so through his disobedience and the subsequent departure of the anointing, back to the grave he went.

Being in the belly of a whale represents being in a pit of death, as we see in the book of Matthew.

Matthew 12:40 KJV
For as Jonah was three days and three nights in the whale's belly, so shall the Son of man be three days and three nights in the heart of the earth.

So Jonah basically went right back to the grave (which is where he had been until Elijah raised him from the dead) until he repented.

But why did Jonah hate the Ninevites so much, and why was he so reluctant to testify to them? Why was a man of his caliber, who had been trained by Elijah and Elisha, behaving this way? Because Jonah had been given a "nevuah", a prophecy, and he knew through the Spirit what the Ninevites were going to do to Israel. He knew that the Ninevites would become part of the Assyrian Empire, and that the Assyrians would scatter the northern kingdom and the 10 tribes of the north. Jonah knew that the Assyrians would destroy the northern kingdom, that they would destroy the land, the trees, the fruit, and that they would burn down the northern kingdom. Jonah knew what they were going to do to Israel in the future and he didn't want to save the lives of the Ninevites. God wanted to give the Ninevites a chance to repent first, but Jonah refused to listen to the Lord.

So God basically said to Jonah, "You were created for this, but you don't want to do what I created you for and you made the choice to refuse your destiny. It's your own choice not to recognize why I raised you from the dead. It's your own choice not to do what I gave you the anointing to do. And there are consequences for your choices."

When the anointing lifts through our blatant disobedience, through our own choices, we go back to where we were before we were anointed. So Jonah was in the belly of a whale for three days and three nights. It was like being in a grave, and we see in Jonah 2 that Jonah repented. Isn't it wonderful how repentance and owning what we've done wrong can switch things back really quickly? Jonah repented, and the whale spewed Jonah out.

Jonah 2:1-2 KJV
[1] Then Jonah prayed unto the Lord his God out of the fish's belly, [2] And said, I cried by reason of mine affliction unto the Lord, and he heard me; out of the belly of hell cried I, and thou heardest my voice.

Jonah 2:9-10 KJV
[9] But I will sacrifice unto thee with the voice of thanksgiving; I will pay that that I have vowed. Salvation is of the Lord. [10] And the Lord spake unto the fish, and it vomited out Jonah upon the dry land.

So how does this account of Jonah apply to our lives, and what spiritual signs do we need to look out for to make sure that we're not falling away from the Lord's plan and destiny for our lives? There are three primary signs that we need to heed.

1. Cutting connection and fleeing direction.

It is incredibly important that we obey the Lord, and not cut connection with Him and flee direction. There are three times in the book of Jonah where scripture tells us that Jonah fled from the presence of the Lord and cut connection with Him (twice in Jonah 1:3 and once in Jonah 1:10).

Jonah 1:3 KJV

But Jonah rose up to flee unto Tarshish from the presence of the Lord, and went down to Joppa; and he found a ship going to Tarshish: so he paid the fare thereof, and went down into it, to go with them unto Tarshish from the presence of the Lord.

Jonah 1:10 KJV

Then were the men exceedingly afraid, and said unto him. Why hast thou done this? For the men knew that he fled from the presence of the Lord, because he had told them.

We need to ask the Lord if we have cut connection with Him in any way, or fled direction from His instructions to us or from His presence.

2. Spiritual stagnation and lack of motivation.

If we see signs of spiritual stagnation and lack of motivation, which can also appear as a spirit of apathy or as sleepiness, we need to get back on track with the Lord. In the following verses, we can see how Jonah's disobedience led to spiritual stagnation and sleepiness.

Jonah 1:4-5 KJV

[4] But the Lord sent out a great wind into the sea, and there was a mighty tempest in the sea, so that the ship was like to be broken. [5] Then the mariners were afraid, and cried every man unto his god, and cast forth the wares that were in the ship into the sea, to lighten it of them. But Jonah was gone down into the sides of the ship; and he lay, and was fast asleep.

3. Descending to a lower level.

We can see how scripture draws a parallel between fleeing from the presence of the Lord, which we saw above three times in Jonah 1:3 and Jonah 1:10, and descending to a lower level, which we see three times in Jonah 1:3 and Jonah 1:5. Scripture is indicating that fleeing from the presence of the Lord and being disobedient is connected with descending spiritually to a lower level of destiny.

Jonah 1:3 KJV

But Jonah rose up to flee unto Tarshish from the presence of the Lord, and went down to Joppa; and he found a ship going to Tarshish: so he paid the fare thereof, and went down into it, to go with them unto Tarshish from the presence of the Lord.

Jonah 1:5b KJV

But Jonah was gone down into the sides of the ship; and he lay, and was fast asleep.

If we know that our lives are not at the level of destiny that the Lord has planned for us, we need to repent and ask God for the grace to fulfill our destinies at the highest level that He intended.

Prayer

Dear Lord,

I ask You that I would behold the sign of the prophet Jonah. You told us that this is the sign that is going to be given, and Lord God, I ask You to help me understand it. Help me understand my calling and my gifts. Help me understand the accountability for what You've trusted into my hands for Your kingdom. Let me fulfill the call of God upon my life, in Jesus' name.

Diary for Destiny

1. Are there any ways that you have cut connection with the Lord? If so, repent and ask the Lord's forgiveness, then ask the Lord what steps He wants you to take.

2. What has the Lord already shown you about His destiny for your life? Are you living in the fullness of His plan for you? If not, what can you do to reach the next level of your destiny?

Chapter 7

Supernatural Sensitivity To The Holy Spirit: Cultivating Clarity

Achieving supernatural sensitivity to the Holy Spirit is one of the most strategic weapons of war in our arsenal against the spirit of Jezebel and seducing spirits of the end times. Supernatural sensitivity to the Holy Spirit and following the leading of the Holy Spirit are some of the most important gifts of grace available to the believer. We need fellowship with the Holy Spirit so that we have the gift of discernment, which is a critical weapon of war against Jezebel. In addition, once you begin to trust the Holy Spirit as your dearest friend and closest treasure, you will never want anything to interrupt that relationship. Beloved, this kind of closeness to Him is the most essential element in the walk of the believer. This is because the Holy Spirit is the only one who can reveal Jesus to us.

When I was a young Christian, I remember being gripped by every word that Kathryn Kuhlman taught. To this day her teaching is one of the most priceless treasures of my life. I recall her saying, "We don't lead the Holy Spirit; we follow Him." She meant that we must learn the art of yielding ourselves over completely to the Holy Spirit. It is the Holy Spirit who is the Spirit of Truth, and He will lead us into all truth (John 16:13). The Spirit of Truth is the one who will enable us to discern between the spirit of truth and the spirit of error (John 4:6).

John 16:13-14 KJV
[13] Howbeit when He, the Spirit of truth, is come, He will guide you into all truth: for He shall not speak of Himself; but whatsoever He shall hear, that shall He speak: and He will shew you things to come. [14] He shall glorify me: for He shall receive of mine, and shall shew it unto you.

The Holy Spirit will never speak of Himself. In the middle part of John 16:13, we see that the Holy

Spirit "shall not speak of Himself; but whatsoever He shall hear, that shall He speak." Beloved, He will only lead the believer to a place of having Jesus, seeing Jesus, loving Jesus, and seeking Jesus.

In John 16:13, Jesus said, "He shall glorify me." John 16:14 says that "He (the Holy Spirit) will take of mine and show it unto you," meaning that the Holy Spirit will only show us Jesus and reveal Jesus to us.

The Holy Spirit is also our teacher. Jesus said, "He shall teach you all things and bring all things to your remembrance that I have said unto you." His words to you, beloved, will be only what Jesus has spoken. Notice that the "words" the Holy Spirit speaks are so united with Jesus that the seven letters to the seven churches in the book of Revelation begin in a unique genre. They begin with Jesus identifying Himself as the one who is speaking. For example, Revelation 2:1 introduces the letter to the church at Ephesus with the words, "These things saith He that holdeth the seven stars," and Revelation 2:18 introduces the letter to the church at Thyatira with the words, "Unto the angel of the church of Thyatira write, These things saith the Son of God." This is the exact pattern of introduction to all seven churches.

The pattern of the close, however, is not signatured the same way it is opened. It opens with Jesus Himself being the one who is addressing the churches, yet it closes with the same signature in all seven letters: "Let him that hath an ear hear what the Spirit saith to the churches."

This means Jesus will only speak through His "voice" here on earth which is the person and power of the Holy Spirit. As believers, we must understand that it is God's perfect, most excellent will that everything we do is through the Holy Spirit. It is God's will that we be skilled and sensitive to the way the Holy Spirit speaks and works. He will never lead us to do something out of the parameters of God's word. He will never glorify a person's carnality or flesh. He desires that we would learn through daily dependence on Him how to do everything exactly as Jesus wants it done. In contrast, false prophets prophesy out of their own hearts and have "seen nothing," as we will see in the following passages of scripture.

Ezekiel 13:3-5 KJV
[3] Thus saith the Lord God; Woe unto the foolish prophets, that follow their own spirit, and have seen nothing! [4] O Israel, thy prophets are like the foxes in the deserts. [5] Ye have not gone up into the gaps, neither made up the hedge for the house of Israel to stand in the battle in the day of the Lord.

The prophet Ezekiel is rebuking the false prophets because they do not provide the word that is able to cause Israel to "stand in the day of battle."

Ezekiel 13:10a KJV
Because, even because they have seduced my people..

Ezekiel 13:6b KJV
They have made others to hope that they would confirm the word.

These texts mean that false prophets will seduce God's people to hope in a false word, usually resulting in confusion, division, or some deceiving device to distract us from our calling.

In Ezekiel 13:9, the text teaches that following false prophets prohibits entrance into the land of promise.

Ezekiel 13:9 KJV
And mine hand shall be upon the prophets that see vanity, and that divine lies: they shall not be in the assembly of my people, neither shall be written in the writing of the house of Israel, neither shall they enter into the land of Israel; and ye shall know that I am the Lord God.

"Neither shall they enter the land" means through false prophets we are disenabled in destiny. We are prohibited from entering the places of promise because they led us astray out of the path God ordained for us.

The Lord also wants us to desire and seek after the gifts of grace that we have no ability to attain in our natural selves. These are the charismatic gifts of grace. These gifts enable us to do what is impossible through our human limitation.

1 Corinthians 14:1 KJV
Follow after charity, and desire earnestly spiritual gifs, but rather that ye may prophesy.

1 Corinthians 12:1 KJV
Now concerning spiritual gifts, brethren, I would not have you ignorant.

God's perfect, most excellent will is that we learn how to prefer what the Holy Spirit wants as most important; thus, we must learn how to follow the promptings and leadings of the Spirit. It is vitally important, beloved readers, that we do this with skill and excellence by becoming educated in the Word of God. The Word of God is one of the most important weapons of war in our battle against the seducing spirits of end times and the spirit of Jezebel. We must devote ourselves to study of God's Word. We must seek after it and spend a lifetime submitting ourselves to it. The following text teaches that one of the signs of the end times will be when mankind will no longer be able to endure sound doctrine.

2 Timothy 4:3-4 KJV
[3] For the time will come when they will not endure sound doctrine: but after their own lusts shall they heap to themselves teachers, having itching ears; [4] And they shall turn away their ears from the truth, and shall be turned unto fables.

Judgment for Jezebel

In Revelation 2:20, the text teaches that the spirit of Jezebel is not a false prophet, but is a seducing spirit of a false prophet. The same word "seduce" is used both in Ezekiel 13:10 and in Revelation 2:20.

Revelation 2:20
Notwithstanding I have a few things against thee, because thou sufferest that woman Jezebel, which calleth herself a prophetess, to teach and to seduce my servants to commit fornication, and to eat things sacrificed unto idols.

According to what Jesus said in Revelation 2:20, Jezebel is a false prophet that seduces through a table prepared with things sacrificed to idols. In a literal sense of scripture, the phrase "to eat things sacrificed to idols" is a direct connect to the book of 1 Kings.

1 Kings 18:19 KJV
Now therefore send, and gather to me all Israel unto mount Carmel, and the prophets of Baal four

hundred fifty, and the prophets of the groves four hundred, which eat at Jezebel's table.

"Eating at Jezebel's table" is spiritually synonymous with "partaking of something." In this case, Jezebel's table is a direct connect to false teaching and erroneous doctrine. This is why we need to not be led astray by a person's "gifts." One of the most dangerous deceptions is following a person only for their gift. A person's gift does not qualify them for ministry. Nowhere in scripture, not on one page, not in one verse, not in one line does the Bible ever use a person's "gift" for the credentials of a call. However, we are easily led astray by titles. The text teaches that what is "gifted" must be "sifted" and perfected to give God the utmost glory.

The spiritual similarities between false prophets and false teachers are of primary concern in the book of 2 Peter.

2 Peter 2:1 KJV
But there were false prophets also among the people, even as there shall be false teachers among you, who privily shall bring in damnable heresies, even denying the Lord that bought them, and bring upon themselves swift destruction.

This is why scripture conveys the need to cultivate clarity in our discernment in 1 John 4:1 and 1 John 4:6.

1 John 4:1 KJV
Beloved, believe not every spirit, but try the spirits whether they are of God: because many false prophets are gone out into the world.

1 John 4:6 KJV
We are of God: he that knoweth God heareth us; he that is not of God heareth not us. Hereby know we the spirit of truth, and the spirit of error.

The way the seducing spirit of Jezebel will lure you out of your place is by "feeding" you at her table. (1 Kings 18:19, Revelation 2:20). Heresy, false doctrine, and the seducing spirit of corrupt counsel are among her serpentine subtleties.

One of the culprit cohorts of the Jezebel spirit is the spirit of Athaliah. Athaliah was also an illegal queen in the southern kingdom of Judah, a few years after Jezebel was queen in the northern kingdom. The culprit cohort of Athaliah was a queen on an assignment to destroy "the seed royal."

2 Chronicles 22:10 KJV
But when Athaliah the mother of Ahaziah saw that her son was dead, she arose and destroyed all the seed royal of the house of Judah.

In a historic sense of scripture, it was only the kings of Judah in the southern kingdom that were anointed as the legitimate king after the time of Jeroboam. In a personal prophetic sense of scripture,

Athaliah was after the seed royal, meaning the seed that was the "anointed." Her objective was to be an anointing assailant and to destroy every one with the potential promise of being king or having the anointing.

In a literal sense of scripture, the context conveys details between Jezebel and Athaliah that are strikingly similar. First, Jezebel and Athaliah are from the same family and have their family origins in Omri. Second, scripture also tells us that Jezebel and Athaliah both gave wicked counsel to their family members.

2 Chronicles 22:3 KJV
He (Ahaziah, the son of Athaliah) also walked in the ways of the house of Ahab: for this mother was his counselor to do wickedly.

1 Kings 21:25 KJV

But there was none like unto Ahab, which did sell himself to do wickedness in the sight of the Lord, whom Jezebel his wife stirred up.

Scripture is drawing a parallel between Jezebel, who gave constant evil counsel to Ahab, and Athaliah, who gave wicked counsel to her son Ahaziah.

The third striking similarity between Athaliah and Jezebel is the poison given by Athaliah to kill the seed royal, and the sustenance that Jezebel provided for the four hundred prophets of the grove who ate at Jezebel's table. In a symbolic sense of scripture, feeding someone is a parallel to feeding them false doctrine, or teaching that is void of the cross, the blood of Jesus, death to self, character, or teaching us how to become more like Jesus. The evil words given by Jezebel at her table and the poison that Athaliah used to murder the seed royal are two devices of deception carefully calculated by both of them. These similarities indicate how the carefully calculated plan of the enemy will divide friendships, divert destinies, pull us out of your God given assignment, and move us away from the anointing and from God's will. The objective is to make us stop serving God. The ploy is to deceive us out of our destiny, oftentimes by making us completely content with compromise.

Here are four ways to cultivate clarity when discerning the spirit of Jezebel:

1. Has there been an unusually long dry period during which you haven't been able to feel or hear from God? Is there no dew or rain of the anointing?

1 King 17:1 KJV
And Elijah the Tishbite, who was of the inhabitants of Gilead, said unto Ahab, As the Lord God of Israel liveth, before whom I stand, there shall not be dew nor rain these years, but according to my word.

The Prophet Elijah shut up the heavens because of Jezebel.

2. If you are in ministry, or if you have just experienced a great victory for the King, have you felt like you are worthless, extremely discouraged, and meant to die?

1 Kings 19:3 KJV
And when he saw that, he arose, and went for his life, and came to Beer-sheba, which belongeth to Judah, and left his servant there.

3. Are you aware of any ungodly agreements or word curses trying to stop you from getting to the next level?

1 Kings 19:1-2 KJV
[1] And Ahab told Jezebel all that Elijah had done, and withal how he had slain all the prophets with the sword. [2] Then Jezebel sent a messenger unto Elijah, saying, So let the gods do to me, and more

also, if I make not thy life as the life of one of them by to morrow about this time.

4. Is the enemy trying manipulation through intimidation?

1 King 21:7 KJV
And Jezebel his wife said unto him, Dost thou now govern the kingdom of Israel? arise, and eat bread, and let thine heart be merry: I will give thee the vineyard of Naboth the Jezreelite.

These spiritual symptoms could very well mean that you are under an oppressive attack of the spirit of Jezebel.

This is why we need the Holy Spirit more than ever before.

Prayer

Dear Lord,

I thank You for the Holy Spirit. I ask You for the gift of discernment and for all the gifts that the Holy Spirit has to give. I give you praise and I give you thanks for the anointing that breaks the yoke. Help me to glorify you in all that I do. With your help, I will fulfill my destiny. In the name of Jesus, amen!

Diary for Destiny

1. What are the different ways that the Holy Spirit has worked in your life? Take some time to thank the Holy Spirit for His presence and activity in your life.

2. What steps will you take to develop a closer relationship with the Holy Spirit?

For a Complete List of Books,
CDs and Ministry Resources by
Dr. Michelle Corral,
Contact:

Breath of the Spirit Prophetic Word Center
P.O. BOX 2676
Orange, CA 92669

Phone # (714) 694-1100

Youtube.com/DrMichelleCorral
Word Network on Mondays
@ 10:30 pm PST
www.breathofthespirit.org
www.drmichellecorral.com
facebook.com/Dr.Corral